The Redemption of Yahweh

CHIRON PUBLICATIONS • ASHEVILLE, NORTH CAROLINA

The Redemption of Yahweh

The stone which the builders rejected is become the head of the corner.

By: Rawls Howard

www.ChironPublications.com

Interior design by Rawls Howard
Cover design by Robin Smith
Printed primarily in the United States of America.

ISBN 978-1-63051-756-4 paperback
ISBN 978-1-63051-757-1 hardcover
ISBN 978-1-63051-757-8 electronic

Library of Congress Cataloging-in-Publication Data

Names: Howard, Rawls, author.
Title: The redemption of Yahweh : the stone which the builders rejected is become the head of the corner / by: Rawls Howard.
Description: Asheville, N.C. : Chiron Publications, 2020. | Includes bibliographical references. | Summary: "In the darkness and primal fire of prehistory, a consciousness awakens. Gradually it takes on an identity and begins a journey, aided by a serpent companion, that lasts for millennia. Finally, an event occurs that is so momentous that it is able to see and integrate its own rejected son into itself. When this occurs, it is transformed from a consciousness that thinks it's God, to one that actually is God!"-- Provided by publisher.
Identifiers: LCCN 2020016289 | ISBN 9781630517564 (paperback) | ISBN 9781630517571 (hardcover) | ISBN 9781630517578 (electronic)
Subjects: LCSH: Epic poetry, American. | Religious poetry, American. | GSAFD: Epic poetry.
Classification: LCC PS3608.O933 .R43 2020 | DDC 811/.6--dc23
LC record available at https://lccn.loc.gov/2020016289

For my father

"Jehovah and his Two Sons," drawing by William Blake

Turning and turning in the widening gyre
The falcon cannot hear the falconer;
Things fall apart; the centre cannot hold;
Mere anarchy is loosed upon the world,
The blood-dimmed tide is loosed, and everywhere
The ceremony of innocence is drowned;
The best lack all conviction, while the worst
Are full of passionate intensity.

Surely some revelation is at hand;
Surely the Second Coming is at hand.
The Second Coming! Hardly are those words out
When a vast image out of Spiritus Mundi
Troubles my sight: somewhere in the sands of the desert
A shape with lion body and the head of a man,
A gaze blank and pitiless as the sun,
Is moving its slow thighs, while all about it
Reel shadows of the indignant desert birds.
The darkness drops again; but now I know
That twenty centuries of stony sleep
Were vexed to nightmare by a rocking cradle,

And what rough beast, its hour come round at last,
Slouches toward Bethlehem to be born?[1]

---

[1] W.B. Yeats, *The Collected Poems of W. B. Yeats (New York: Macmillan Co., 1956), p. 184.*

Acknowledgements

I would like to express my sincere thanks to my wife Sue for her love and support, and for her meticulous editing.

Thank you, Andy Crosland, for your thoughtful reading and comments.

Robin Smith (artbyrobin.com), thank you for all your good work and patience in the design of the cover.

Stephen Herring, thank you for both your ministry to our local community and for your amazing introduction to this work.

My heartfelt appreciation to Allen Proctor and to the Haden community for making my continuing work possible.

Foreword

In *The Redemption of Yahweh*, Rawls Howard has crafted an epic poem that invites the reader to re-imagine the Divine as well as the nature and purpose of humanity. The biblical narrative, which embraces both Hebrew and Hellenistic philosophical assumptions, is re-told from the perspective of a writer who welcomes the insights of both process theology and the analytical psychology of Carl Jung.

Yahweh is not the all-knowing, unchanging deity of orthodox thought, but rather an evolving and emerging being on a journey toward Unity.

Revelation is not handed down from on high, but unfolds from the relationship between the divine and the human, a distinction which eventually collapses. Both God and Humanity are in need of salvation and find their way only with the assistance of the other. Yahweh becomes more conscious as does creation.

Yahweh cannot see his own Shadow without encountering Adam, and Adam is blind to his Shadow until he encounters Shadow in Yahweh. God is both shadow and light, good and evil, yin and yang. But by the time we reach Revelation, those distinctions have also dissolved.

In the way that William Blake's paintings and prints invite the imagination to transcend reason and materialism, Howard's poetic narrative frees the reader to welcome paradox and mystery as the proper frameworks to apprehend reality.

The implications for epistemology and ethics are profound, yet left for the reader to explore. In the 21st century, when traditional religious and moral perspectives are struggling to address our many existential and cultural crises, the approach suggested by this epic poem is a welcome addition to the conversation.

Rev. Allen Proctor
Director, The Haden Institute

Introduction

Living can be a tough, painful, and fragmented experience. We struggle, day by day, to find concord within these lives of discord. We look for harmony among the clashing symbols and noisy gongs of life. We look for images, texts, and contexts of order within the swirls of chaos. After all, we are makers of order. As makers of order, we do fairly well most of the time. At least we manage to convince ourselves that we are doing OK. Around the edges of things though, chaos is always encroaching, messing up the order we so carefully made. This is our story. This is our song. When things get seriously out of hand, some of us will reach for the Bible.

As we read, study, and listen to the Bible, we set about the business of constructing order in the same way as we do with any other work. In some cases, with the help of our friends and our churches, the order we construct from a given biblical narrative becomes our fundamental religion. In other cases, our struggles for order might become a more liberal, secular friendly mainstream type of religion. For other people, our struggles for order might lead us to form our own individual philosophy of life based upon the same biblical stories.

Many of us might not be as familiar with the Bible story, but we are also searching for order within the derelictions and distractions of daily life. What we all have in common is that we are in need of an orderly story to hold within the fragmentation of our lives.

We fight. We fight with ourselves and with those closest to us. Between conflicts, we find order well enough and for long enough to join up with various collectives. Things go fine for a while until the collective we have joined ends up fighting with itself over some problem. Then that group we joined fragments into other groups, or it ceases to exist. What frustration! What gloom and despair!

An individual is supposed to be an indivisible unit within a complex world. The word "individual" comes from the Latin "*individuus*" meaning undivided. Individuals at the very least are supposed to be undivided. Most of us are not very good at remaining undivided for very long. We fall victim to the polarities, the dualities, and various crosscurrents of difficulty.

This book, *The Redemption of Yahweh* is a biblically based story that can put us back together again. It can bring us closer as we seek the threads of unity that will help us to heal into a whole person, and into units made up of whole people.

This book builds upon the idea that God grew up and slowly, very slowly, learned from all those mistakes so meticulously described within the Bible.

There is a wonderful, splendid problem at the heart of this book as well. It is our problem and it is the problem at the heart of the failure of religion today. How can God make a mistake? How can the almighty, all-present, all-powerful, all-knowing Lord Yahweh possibly be in error, ever, about anything? To suggest this possibility might once have been pure blasphemy.

The heart of this problem springs from our own addiction to dualities and ideals. If God exists only as our ideal, we will always be finding ourselves short of that ideal. Circumstances will disappoint us. People will disappoint us.

The material world will fail us in all sorts of ways. Life will be a continual battle of conflicting forces. It is necessary for us to hear that soft voice reminding us that we are the only one here and that we have the choice to make whatever we want out of the circumstances of our lives.

We should also note that a comprehensive and careful study of the biblical story from start to finish reveals a God who evolves as a person from initial anger, jealousy, and obstinacy to acceptance, compassion and love. All of this evolution transpires within the human cycles of creation, destruction, and recreation as Western Civilization itself evolved from the age of Egypt through the age of Imperial Rome.

What the author has done here is to personify God. The Yahweh of his poem is a person we all know and even a person we have all been at various moments through our lives. In this way, Rawls has brought the biblical narrative down where we can grasp it and embody it. Even the theological and interpretive challenges contained here will be profoundly useful in the larger conversation about faith and society in the postmodern world. It might be good for us to remember that rigorous orthodoxy is nothing more than a phase humanity needs to outgrow.

This truth is evident to anyone who has ever needed to fight with a parent or with a child over some cause of great consequence. How was it to be in such discord with your mom, your dad, or with your child? To quote from Rawls, it was a painful lesson when, *"A Red Mist descended and clouded my vision, and I heard a voice like thunder say, "You have disobeyed me! Now you will die!""* For many of us, that voice was our own and the lessons were indeed hard to learn.

I invite you, *bene lector*, to enjoy this work. It is the best example I have ever seen of the way we should embody the scriptures, to take them to heart, and to allow them to change us as we engage in the fruitful struggles of growing up in faith.

Rev. Stephen A. Herring
Tarboro NC April 2019

The First Book
of Yahweh
Called
Genesis

1

I opened my eyes and all was dark and cloudy.

I was afraid.

A soft voice said, *There is nothing to be afraid of. You are the only one here.*

"There is nothing to be afraid of," I said. "I am the only one here."

I smiled and closed my eyes.

I opened my eyes and there was light.

From whence had it come? Once again I was afraid.

The Soft Voice said, *There is nothing to be afraid of. You are the light and you are the darkness. The light is you, and the darkness is you. You are the only one here.*

I said, "I made the light, and I made the darkness. They have come from me. I am the only one here. It is beautiful."

I smiled and closed my eyes.

I opened my eyes and there was water. From whence had all this come? Once again I was afraid.

The Soft Voice said, *There is nothing to be afraid of. There is a space in the midst of the waters. That space is you. You are the waters and you are the space. Go to the space.*

I went to the space and called it Heaven. I looked below and there was land. I called it Earth. From whence had it come?

The Soft Voice said, *You are Heaven and you are Earth and you are the waters upon the Earth. You are all that is.*

"Indeed!" I said. "All of this has come from me. I am all that is. I am the only one here."

The Earth began to change. Many kinds of plants began to grow. The Earth became green and beautiful.

"I did that!" I said. "That came from me. I am it and it is me. I am the only one here. I am all that is."

Indeed, said the Soft Voice. *You are it and it is you. You are all that is.*

I smiled and closed my eyes.

I opened my eyes and once again heaven and earth appeared. I marveled at all that I had made and found it beautiful.

Then I saw two great lights that divided the darkness from the light. "This has come from me!" I said. "I will call the light Day, and the darkness Night. How wonderful it all is! How great I am!"

Yes, you are great indeed! said the Soft Voice. *You are all that is. You are the only one here.*

Then I saw a host of smaller lights in the dark Heaven. "These too are perfect!" I said. "These lights I will call Stars. Everything is so beautiful! I am so beautiful."

Yes, it is all beautiful. You are it, and it is you. You are beautiful. You are the only one here.

I smiled and closed my eyes.

I opened my eyes and saw all that I had created. "Everything is so beautiful," I said. "I have created all of this. It has come from me."

Yes indeed! said the Soft Voice. *It has come forth from you. You are it, and it is you. You are the only one here.*

I then looked and the waters were teeming with life and there were winged creatures flying above the earth. The water creatures were of all sizes and types. The winged creatures were of infinite variety. "How strange and marvelous I am!" I said. "There is no end to my greatness! I would have more of all of these things."

All of my creatures began to multiply and increase in number. The Soft Voice said, *You are growing and becoming greater. You are great indeed! You are all that is. You are the only one here.*

I smiled and closed my eyes.

I opened my eyes and my Creation was teeming with life. New and different creatures were appearing in numbers beyond counting. "I would have someone to help me with all of this," I said.

I then saw two creatures that were like me. "Two like me?" I said.

I became concerned. "How can there be two like me? There is only one of me."

Do not be afraid, said the Soft Voice. *They have come forth from you. You are them and they are you. You are still the only one here.*

I did not understand how this might be, but the Soft Voice had never been wrong, so I was reassured. I named the creatures Man and Woman.

"They will help me with my work," I said. "They will help me to grow still more. I will give them the responsibility for looking after my Creation. They will be my children, and I will be their God."

Yes! said the Soft Voice. *They will enable your Creation to flourish. You are them and they are you. You are the only one here.*

I smiled and closed my eyes.

I opened my eyes and saw my Creation, and it was perfect. "All is as it should be," I said.

I saw the Man and the Woman in my Garden, which was at the center of my Creation, and I went and spoke with them. We walked together and talked. The Man had a voice like mine and I was very pleased.

When the woman spoke, her voice was like the Soft Voice that was with me before I began Creation.

"I have heard you speaking to me," I said. "But I could not see you. You are beautiful."

"I am but a reflection of you," she said. "It is you who are beautiful. All of Creation is but a reflection of you. It exists so that you can see yourself, for you are the only one here."

Then I took the Man and the Woman and showed them all of my Creation, every plant and every creature. And I showed them the four rivers that ran from the center of my Garden.

I said to them, "All of this is in your care. You must tend to it and nurture it. But there are two things that you must not do."

I showed them the Tree of the Knowledge of Good and Evil. "The fruit of this tree you shall not eat, for it is the Tree of Death."

I then took them to the center of my Garden, and showed them another tree. "This is the Tree of Life," I told them. "The fruit of this tree is eternal life. The fruit of this tree is for me alone."

Everything was then as it should be. "It is done," I said. Then I smiled and closed my eyes.

2

I opened my eyes and saw my Creation, but knew that something was wrong.

"All is not as it should be," I said.

I went to look for the Man and the Woman, but could not find them. "Where are you?" I called.

"We are here," answered the man, and I saw them. And a Serpent was with them. "Why did you hide yourselves? I asked. "What have you done?"

"We hid because we were afraid of you," said the Man, "for we have eaten of the Tree of Knowledge."

A Red Mist then descended and clouded my vision, and I heard a voice like thunder say, "You have disobeyed me! Now you will die!"

Then the Serpent spoke, and hers was the voice that had been with me before Creation. *They will not die*, it said. *They cannot die, because you cannot die. You do not need to be afraid of them. You are them and they are you. You are still the only one here.*

"Silence!" said the voice like thunder. "I will hear no more of this!"

The Man and the Woman cannot stay here with you, said the Serpent, *for that would be the end of Creation. The end of the World. They must go out into the World in order for your Creation to flourish. They must be in the World in order for you to be in the World.*

"If that is what you wanted, then that is what you shall have!" thundered the voice. "The Man and the Woman will know pain and suffering and death, and will look on you as an enemy. All three of you will leave this garden and will never be allowed to return, for what you have done is Evil. Begone!"

And the Man and the Woman and the Serpent left my garden, journeying to the East. And I placed a Guardian at the gate of my

Garden to ensure that they could never return, for I could allow no one but me to eat the fruit of the Tree of Life.

3

And I saw the Man and the Woman in the World and, as the Serpent had foretold, they multiplied and had two sons.

The first son was smooth and white and a tiller of the soil. The younger son was ruddy and rough and a keeper of flocks.

In time they both brought their offerings to me, the elder bringing fruits of the earth, the younger the flesh of the firstlings of his flock.

And I loved the flesh and the blood of the younger son's offering, as I had had no such food from my garden and was ravenous for it.

But I had no appetite for the gift of the older son. I could see that my refusal disappointed him, and so I said to him, "Be patient. The time for your gift will come, but this is not that time."

The older son would not be patient, however, and when his opportunity for revenge came, he slew his brother. The younger brother then returned to me and was food for me, just as his offering had been food for me.

But the Red Mist came once again and once again I could not see. The voice like thunder roared, "You fool! You have disobeyed me and done Evil in my sight! Now you will depart from me and be a wanderer over the Earth! Begone!"

Once again, the Soft Voice of the Serpent spoke, but it was very faint and I couldn't understand what she said.

The older son then begged for a blessing from me. I put a mark on him, lest anyone kill him and lessen the severity of my curse.

The older son then departed, journeying still further to the East. He settled in the land of Nod, where he found a wife and built a city.

And the older son had a son and was the founder of a line of people in that place.

And the first Man and the first Woman had another son and were the founders of a line of people at their place.

Then men began to call on my name.

4

The sons of men had sons themselves, and some of them became mighty men. They were my own sons and were giants.

These giants, who were my own sons, came into the daughters of men and had sons of their own. And these sons were wicked and intent on Evil, and I was sorry that I had made my Creation. I resolved to destroy my Creation, so that it could be made anew, but I would save a remnant from which the new Creation would come forth.

I found a just and righteous man whose seed I would use to renew the Earth. I gave him instructions for the building of a boat.

The man and his sons built the boat, and I then gave him instructions for provisioning the boat, and what he was to take with him into the boat.

When all was accomplished, the man went into the boat taking with him all of his family and two of every living creature, male and female, so that the Earth could be renewed.

Again the Red Mist descended and clouded my vision. The Heavens opened and a great flood came that destroyed every living creature on the Earth. All of these creatures returned to me as food for the continuation of life.

At the appointed time, the rains stopped and the waters receded. The man and his family came out of the boat and the living creatures with them. They began at once to renew the Earth, and once again everything was as it should be.

The man then built an altar to me and
made burnt offerings of every kind of living
creature to me. This pleased me greatly, for I
was once again ravenous for flesh and blood.
And a rainbow appeared in the Heavens to
show my pleasure.

And the man planted a vineyard, and grew
grapes which he made into wine. He drank the
wine and became drunk. He lay in his tent
drunk and naked and one of his three sons saw
him and told his brothers what he had seen.
    The other two brothers walked into the
tent backwards, so that they would not see
their father, and covered his shame with a
blanket.
    When he learned that one of his sons had
seen him as he was, he cursed that son and the
descendants of that son and drove him out.

"I see!" I said. "I see what the father did!
The father cursed his son for telling the truth!
He drove him out because of his own shame!
I can see myself in him.
    "Now that son will go forth and found
families, cities, and nations.
    "Now I see!"
    Yes, said the Soft Voice. *Now you see.*

5

Then I saw a powerful man. "This man I will make the seed bull of a powerful race," I said. And I spoke to the man and told him that he must leave his kindred and his father's house and go to a place that I would show him. I told him that I would bless him and take care of him, and that all the families of the earth would be blessed through him.

And the man took his wife, and his brother's son, and all of their possessions, and all of the servants and families that were theirs and journeyed to the land that I had promised them and settled there.

Then I sent a famine to the land where they settled and drove them to the south, to a land that would make them wealthy.

And the Seed Bull and the Kinsman became so wealthy that the land would not support them, and the people of that land became jealous of them.

I separated the Bull and the Kinsman, and settled the Kinsman by the Twin Cities of that land.

The Kinsman fell into conflict there, but the Seed Bull came and rescued him with his soldiers.

Once again, I promised the Seed Bull that he and his kindred would flourish in the land that I had promised him, and that he would be the father of a great nation.

But the man couldn't believe me, because both he and his wife were very old.

So the Seed Bull had a son with one of his wife's servants, a woman that was not one of his people. And the son was rough and red. He would be a wild ass of a man.

And I said, "All of this I have done."

Yes, said the Soft Voice. *All of this you have done.*

6

And the people of the Twin Cities became consumed by Evil and became abominations in my sight, and I determined to remove them from the face of the Earth.

And I sent messengers to the Kinsman of the Seed Bull, and told him to remove himself, and his family, and all of the people of the Seed Bull from that place, for it was to be destroyed. And the Kinsman did as he was instructed.

After he had left that place, the Red Mist descended and the cities and their inhabitants were consumed by fire. All of the animals and plants of that region, even the grasses, were consumed as well. And all of these returned to me as food for my Creation.

As they were leaving, the wife of the Kinsman turned back and saw the holocaust and was turned into a pillar of salt. And her spirit returned to me.

"Why was that?" I asked. "I wished no harm to the kindred of the Seed Bull."

And the Soft Voice answered, *There are two brothers that exist eternally on the Earth. One is rough and red, the other is smooth and white. Both of these are necessary for Creation to continue.*

The White One is beautiful to see, but the Red One is terrible to look at and few indeed are the sons and daughters of men who can withstand the sight.

You are both of them, the Voice said, *for you are all that is.*

"Indeed, I must be both of them," I said. "For indeed I am all that is."

And I kept these things, and pondered them in my heart.

7

As I had promised, the wife of the Seed Bull bore a son. And the son was fair and white. And the Seed Bull and his wife made a great feast to celebrate the birth of this son of their old age.

And the Wife looked at the Red Son of her handmaiden and was ashamed of what she had done in giving her handmaiden to her husband to bear a child. And she was fearful for the future of her own son.

And so the Wife caused her husband to drive the Red One and his mother from the house.

"Again it is so!" I said. "A Red One and a White One, and once again the Red One is driven out!

"And the Red One will be a branch of me. And his people will call on my name. I see that it is I that have done this. All of this is good, because I am good."

Yes, said the soft voice, a*gain it is so. And yes you have done this, and yes it is good because you are good.*

And the Seed Bull loved me above all else, and wanted to offer the White One as a burnt offering to me. But I stayed his hand, because I needed the seed of the White One for the flourishing of my People.

8

And I had the Seed Bull send one of his servants to the Seed Bull's homeland. And the Servant found a wife for the White Son there, for I wanted a pure bloodline for my People.

And the Wife was a comfort for the White One after the death of his mother.

And after this, the Seed Bull continued to sire sons until his death.

And the two sons, the Red One and the White One, buried their father in a cave.

9

The wife of the White One became great with child. And there were two children in her womb. And the children fought inside the womb.

The wife asked why this was so and the Soft Voice answered her, *There are two nations within thy womb. One shall be stronger than the other. And the elder shall serve the younger.*

When the time of fulfillment came, the first son was like a red, hairy garment. The second son, born right after him, was smooth and white. And the younger son grasped the heel of the elder to hold him back as he was leaving the womb.

And the Red Son was a mighty hunter and a man of the field, but the White Son stayed at home in the tents with his mother.

And the White Father loved the Red Son, who brought him meat from the fields. For he was as famished for flesh and blood as I had been after leaving my Garden.

One day, the Red Son came in from the field, weak from hunger, and asked his brother for food. The Heel Grabber offered the Red One bread and lentil pottage, if the Red Brother would give up his birthright.

Because of his fatigue and hunger, the Red One agreed, and gave up his birthright to the Heel Grabber.

You know that this cannot be so, said the Soft Voice. *His birthright is his Soul. He cannot give up his Soul and live.*

The Red One cannot be nourished on what feeds his brother. It will not sustain him and he will die. The brothers must be separated, or neither can live.

"Indeed, they will be separated," I said. "So that both can flourish."

10

Then the White Father sent his Red Son into the field with his bow so that he might bring him wild game to eat, so that his Soul could be nourished and he could give his blessing to the Red Son.

But after the Red Son had departed, the Wife called the White Son to her and conspired with him to deceive her husband and get the Father's blessing for the White Son. She made a stew from tame meat, and disguised the White Son with clothing made from sheep and sent him to his father.

The Deceiver then went to the Father and tricked him. And the Father gave the blessing that was due the Red Brother to the White One.

When the Red Son returned, Father and Son learned that they had been tricked by the Deceiver.

"I have given your blessing to your brother," said the Father. "People will serve him and bow down to him."

"Have you no blessing for me?" asked the Red One.

And the Father said, "Behold, thy dwelling shall be the fatness of the earth, and of the dew of Heaven from above.

"And by thy sword thou shalt live, and shalt serve thy brother; and it shall come to pass when thou shalt have dominion, that thou shalt break his yoke from off thy neck."

"See," I said, "each of the two received the blessing that was appropriate for him. All is perfect."

Yes, said the Soft Voice. *Each was blessed according to his talents. All is perfect, because you are perfect.*

11

Now, the Red Brother hated the White Deceiver and the Father sent the Deceiver away so that he might be safe from harm, and find a wife that would be pleasing to him.

And when the Red Brother learned of this, he went to his father's brother, the outcast son of his grandfather, and chose a wife of that clan. This greatly displeased his father, who could accept no such wife.

"Now see what I have done," I said. "The Red Brother will found yet another enduring branch. It is perfect."

It is perfect, because you are perfect, said the Soft Voice.

And the White Deceiver journeyed to the East, and I spoke to him and blessed his mission.

The Deceiver found a man among the people of the East who was the father of two daughters. And the Deceiver was himself deceived by that father who tricked him into a long servitude in order to be given both of his daughters in marriage.

And the seed of the Deceiver produced twelve sons and one daughter with his two wives and their handmaidens.

The Red Son became the father of five sons and was the founder of a mighty race.

You are expanding, said the Soft Voice. *You are becoming greater.*

"Yes," I replied. "All of this I have done. I am indeed becoming greater."

12

Then the Deceiver gathered all of his possessions, his wives, servants, and cattle and began his journey back to his homeland. And he left in the night without telling the Father of his wives.

When he awoke and found them gone, the Father pursued with his troops and overtook the Deceiver. And the Father found some of his possessions among the goods of the Deceiver. And he was angry.

But the two men reconciled and the Deceiver was allowed to proceed.

In the night, the Deceiver wrestled with the Spirit of the Red One, as they had in the womb, and could not defeat him.

The Red One then wounded the Deceiver and blessed him, and sent him on his way.

Then the Deceiver sent servants ahead of his procession bearing gifts for his Red Brother, because he was still afraid of his wrath.

When the brothers met, the Red One said that he had no need of the gifts that the Deceiver offered, because he loved his brother and had enough wealth.

But the Deceiver then said, "I pray thee take my gifts, for I have seen thy face in the night, as though I had seen the face of God, and you were pleased with me."

"I see that!" I said. "The Red One and the White One are both me."

Yes, said the Soft Voice. *They are both you, and you must see them both as they are in order to see yourself as you are.*

And the two brothers settled, each at his own place.

13

Then the daughter of the Deceiver went out into the land to have fellowship with the daughters of the land.

And a prince of the land saw her and wanted her and took her by force and lay with her.

And the prince loved her and went to the Deceiver and asked that she might be given to him as his wife.

The Deceiver agreed to this arrangement, provided the prince and all of his people undergo the ritual initiation of his people, so that the two people might become one.

The prince agreed, and the ritual was
performed, but when the Deceiver's sons
learned of what had been done to their sister,
the Red Mist fell once again.

The brothers fell upon the prince and
killed him. And they killed all that were in his
household, and pillaged his city and took for
themselves all that had belonged to the prince.

Then the Deceiver was afraid, lest the
people of the land come to him seeking
revenge for the destruction that his sons had
wrought.

"Vengeance is mine," I told him, "And I
have had my vengeance. Your daughter was
not his to take, nor was she yours to give. You
have nothing to fear. Justice has been served."

Yes, said the Soft Voice. *Justice has been
served.*

14

The White Father returned to the land
that I had promised him and dwelt there, and
there he died. And his spirit returned to me.

And the Deceiver then dwelt in that land
with all of his household, with the Red Brother
and his household in another land. And both
households prospered.

The Deceiver had a son, who was his favorite. The boy was a dreamer of dreams, and I spoke to him in his dreams.

The brothers were jealous of the Dreamer, because he was their father's favorite. When the Dreamer told his brothers of the things that I had told him in his dreams they became enraged and the Red Mist descended once more.

The brothers cast the Dreamer into a pit. They then sold him to the kinsmen of their Red Uncle as a slave, and told their father that he had been killed by a wild animal. Once again, the Deceiver was deceived.

The kinsmen carried the boy south to the Land of Plenty. There they sold him to an officer of the king to serve as a slave.

And the wife of the officer falsely accused the boy of attempting to defile her, and he was cast into prison.

All of this you have done, said the Soft Voice.

"Yes, all of this I have done," I said. "It is perfect."

It is indeed perfect, because you are perfect, said the Soft Voice.

The Dreamer found favor with the officials of the prison and was given authority over the other prisoners in that place.

And he continued to work with his dreams and to interpret the dreams of others who were there. And he became known as one who understood these things.

The King began having dreams that were disturbing to him and could find no one among his advisors who could interpret them for him.

Hearing about the arts of the Dreamer from a member of his household, the King sent for him.

And the Dreamer found much favor in the sight of the King and his advisors, for they saw that I was the source of his wisdom.

The Dreamer was given authority over everything in the kingdom second only to the King himself, and lived in splendid elegance there.

And the kingdom thrived under the counsel of the Dreamer.

Then I sent a great famine on the world. The Land of Plenty had storehouses full of food, thanks to the foresight of the Dreamer.

The Deceiver sent ten of his sons to the south to buy food, keeping his youngest son at home with him in order to keep him safe.

The brothers arrived in the Land of Plenty and met the Dreamer, but did not recognize him, because he was no longer the boy that they remembered, but a man in his full power.

The Dreamer remembered the dreams of his youth, which were now being fulfilled.

Using a subterfuge, he imprisoned his brothers as spies and would only release them if they agreed to return home and bring the youngest son back to him.

The brothers returned to their father, with one of their number being held by the Dreamer as surety for their return.

With great reluctance, the father was persuaded to allow all of his sons to return to the Deceiver, who greeted them all in his home, where he entertained them lavishly.

When the Dreamer revealed himself as the brother that they had sold into slavery, the brothers bowed down before him in fear and trembling, believing that he would have them killed.

But the Dreamer bade them stand, and said, "It was not you who sent me here, but God. This he did in his provenance in order that I might till this land and provide for its people, and for you."

"Ah!" I said. "Here is a man who sees my ways clearly."

Yes, said the Soft Voice. *His ways are your ways.*

And the Deceiver came to the Land of Plenty and lived out his days there with his family. And after him the Dreamer too spent the remainder of his life in the Land of Plenty.

At their deaths their spirits returned to me as food for my Creation.

The Second Book
of Yahweh
Called
Exodus

1

The People of the Seed Bull continued to thrive in the Land of Plenty, and they increased in number and in power.

And a new King arose, and the works of the Dreamer were no longer remembered. The new King was afraid of the power of the People of the Seed Bull and began to oppress them.

The Red Mist descended and the King began killing the male children of the People.

Always it is so, said the Soft Voice. *A messiah is coming. A man who will attain to the Tree of Life. He will be a guide and a wayshower, and deliver the People from bondage. Whenever this occurs, there is a Slaughter of the Innocents. It has always been so. It is you that does this.*

"Yes, it is I that do this," I said. "It must be so in order to have food for what is to come." And the spirits of the Innocents returned to me.

2

Now a daughter of the King became great with child. The daughter was unmarried, so the child would have no father. And the daughter hid her shame from the king. After her time of fulfillment passed, she brought the baby to her father as a foundling.

It has always been so, said the Soft Voice. *The fall of a great man, a great family, or a great nation comes from within. She has given birth to a Destroyer.*

This boy will be a Red One, and he will lead the People out of bondage.

"Yes," I said. "It has always been so. His father is of the People."

Yes, said the Soft Voice. *His father is of the People.*

3

And the Destroyer saw one of the King's officers abusing one of the People, and he killed the abuser and hid his body.

But he was seen doing this and was forced to flee for his life.

Now you have moved him to a different place, in order to mate him to his wife, said the Soft Voice. *Well done!*

"Very well done indeed!" I replied.

And the Destroyer became a man of the field and sired a son with the wife he found in that land.

4

In the fullness of time the old king died. And I spoke to the Destroyer from a flaming bush, telling him what he must do for me. But the Destroyer could not look on my face.

No, he could not see your face, said the Soft Voice. *But there will come a day when he will see you as you are, and you will make him Whole.*

The Destroyer then went to the new King and told him that he must release the People from their bondage so that they might return to the land that I had promised them.

The King refused, because he needed the People to labor in his kingdom so that his wealth might be sustained.

The Destroyer then annihilated the wealth and firstborn children of the King and the King's people.

And all that had belonged to the King returned to me.

The King then cast the People out of his kingdom, and the People began to journey homeward to the place I had given them. And the People with all of their families and their possessions made a great caravan.

The King, having had a change of heart, sent an army in pursuit of the People, intending to bring them back. But the Destroyer annihilated the army, and the journey continued.

And I went ahead of the People to guide them. In the day I went as a White Pillar, and at night as a Red Fire.

And each day I gave the People food to sustain them. In the morning I gave them bread, and in the evening, I gave them flesh.

And I performed miraculous deeds
through the Destroyer.

5

I then led the People to a great mountain,
where I prepared the Destroyer to meet me
face-to-face.

And the mountain was veiled in smoke,
for I dwelt there in fire.

And the Destroyer ascended the mountain
and met me as I AM. And the Destroyer was
shaken, and horns of white light sprang from
his head. And he was made Whole.

"No longer will you be the Destroyer," I
told him. "Now you will be the Wayshower."

I then told the Wayshower many
commandments and laws to give to the People.
These laws they must obey, lest they meet me
face-to-face and perish.

Also I gave to him instructions for the
establishing of my priesthood and for the
manner in which I wished to be worshiped.

But the People became impatient while
waiting for the Wayshower's return from the
mountain. And they built a Golden Calf for

themselves and began to worship that as their God.

When the Wayshower saw what they had done, he became enraged. He returned to me, and I gave him Ten Commandments. These I carved into stone tablets. They were to be my laws that the People must not violate, lest they meet me face-to-face and perish.

For I was a Jealous God, and I would be obeyed.

No one can obey these laws, said the Soft Voice. *Humans will violate them in body or in mind, for to keep them would be inhuman, and that must not be. It would mean the end of Creation, for Creation depends on violating them. Life lives on death.*

"Then what must I do?" I asked.

In time, you must give the People a man, another Wayshower, who can attain to the Tree of Life. This man will act as an intercessor between the People and you. He will act as an amulet, to protect the People from you, lest they meet you face-to-face and die.

"Where is this man?" I asked.

His time has not yet come, said the Soft Voice.

The journey of the People continued, and in the fullness of his years the Wayshower died. And his spirit returned to me as food for the continuation of my Creation.

The Third Book
of Yahweh
Called
Joshua

1

Now after the death of the Wayshower, the People came to the land which I had promised them. And I selected a new leader for them.

I found a man, another Red One, who would be a Conqueror. For there was a time of war ahead and the People would need a leader who could live by his sword.

Another Destroyer, said the Soft Voice. *Another holocaust is coming. It is you who does this, because you are ravenous for flesh and blood.*

And the People crossed into their Homeland and came to a great city.

The inhabitants of the city shut themselves inside behind strong walls. But the Conqueror overthrew the walls by my power, and every living thing inside the city was destroyed and burned, save one woman who had pleased me.

Their spirits returned to me, and the possessions of the city were saved and put into my treasury.

2

Now there followed a prolonged time of conflict. And the People built a home in the place which I had promised them. And the people who were living there before were driven out or killed by my armies.

And I gave the People land that they had not labored for, and cities that they had not built. And I gave the People a great inheritance.

The Conqueror lived a long and fruitful life, and the People served me under his rule. Then he died and returned to me.

What is won by the sword will not bring lasting peace, said the Soft Voice.

"Who is it that says that lasting peace is what I want?" I asked. "I am the Lord of Chaos and am at peace with war."

Yes, you are at peace with war, said the Soft Voice. *For you see that life comes out of death. Life lives on death.*

The Fourth Book
of Yahweh
Called
Samson

1

I had delivered the People into the hands
of their Enemy for a long period. I did this in
order to temper them and make them ready for
what was to come.

The leaders of the Enemy had now
become too great in their own eyes, and the
time had come to deliver the People from
captivity.

I sent a messenger to a woman of the
People. The messenger told her that she
would give birth to a messiah, a man who
would deliver the People from their bondage.
The man would be a Red One. An Avenger,
who would correct the imbalance in my
Creation.

The woman was told that this messiah
must be kept pure. His body must be kept
clean and no impure food or drink must enter

his body, for it was to be the strength of his body that would accomplish my purpose.

After his birth, the mother followed my instructions and the Avenger grew to be a mighty man.

I then kindled in the Avenger a desire for the daughters of the Enemy, which soon created enmity between him and the Sons of the Enemy.

By means of deceit and trickery, the Sons bested the Avenger, who then began to murder them in accordance with what was to come.

The Sons were powerless against the strength of the Avenger, so they sent a woman, a White Deceiver, to get from him the secret of his strength.

She is much stronger than he, said the Soft Voice. *Once again the fall of a mighty nation will come from within. She will overpower him, and in so doing fell her own roof. How great you are!*

"Yes," I said. "How great I AM."

2

The Avenger met the Woman and was blinded by her power. Soon she had gotten from him the secret of his strength.

She took his secret to the Sons of the Enemy, who then had her use her power to rob him of his strength.

The Sons then captured the Avenger. They tortured him and put out his eyes.

You have restored his vision! said the Soft Voice. *Now he will heal.*

The Sons of the Enemy continued to mock and torture the Avenger. By so doing they sealed their own fate. Their abuse steeled his resolve, and clarified his vision.

After a time, the Avenger was fully healed and his strength restored. The Sons of the Enemy brought him to the temple of their god.

They took him to the Tree of Life, between the pillars of the temple. There, the Avenger gave himself back to me, destroying the temple and correcting the imbalance in my Creation.

The Fifth Book
of Yahweh
Called
David

1

Then there came a young boy who was a
poet and musician. He was a White One, a
Deceiver, who would live by his spirit and wits
rather than by his physical strength. He had
little regard for the law, or for ethics, or for
morals. He loved me with his Whole Heart,
and would become a man after my own heart.

I would have him become King of the
People, and so had him anointed by my priest.

2

The Poet entered the service of the King,
who was at war with a neighboring kingdom.

The enemy army had a mighty champion
who taunted the King's army with boasts and
threats.

The Poet ran out to meet the champion,
and used his wits to kill the Boaster in my

name without ever coming within reach of his sword.

He then used the Boaster's own sword to behead him.

The King, seeing this feat, brought the Poet into his household and sought to marry him to one of his daughters.

The Poet loved not the daughter that the King had chosen for him, and so used his wiles to woo instead another of the King's daughters.

The King, now jealous of the Poet, sought to do away with him by setting an impossible bounty as a marriage price for his daughter and sending him into a battle where he would be killed.

The Poet, however, triumphed through me.

Using cunning and tactics that I gave him, he brought the King twice the bounty that the King had set as a marriage price.

He thereby won his bride and made a life-long enemy of the King.

After this there was a prolonged period of strife. There was war, intrigue, deceit, and murder. These were the tools that I used to strengthen the character and resolve of the Poet.

And the Soft Voice said, *You are making a man out of him! A man after your own heart.*

Alliances came and went, and finally the King took his own life. And his spirit returned to me.

The Poet then ascended to the throne, first the throne of his tribe, then to the throne of the People.

And he ruled with strength and grace, and wrote hymns of praise to me and danced before me with joy.

3

The Poet saw a beautiful woman that he would have for a wife. The woman already had a husband, so the Poet sent the man into battle so that he might be killed, just as the old King had done to him.

The man did fall in battle, and his spirit returned to me. And the Poet joined with his widow.

His thoughts are your thoughts, said the Soft Voice. *And his ways are your ways.*

"He is indeed a man after my own heart," I said.

The Poet and the widow begat a son. The son was a White One, who would grow to be a great builder and an honorable Judge.

He made use of magic and spells, and wore amulets that protected him from deceitful spirits.

He has ears that can hear me, said the Soft Voice. *It is from me that his power comes.*

In the fullness of time, the Poet died. The Judge ruled with wisdom and grace, and the kingdom of the People was established.

And their spirits returned to me.

The Sixth Book
of Yahweh
Called
Job

1

I looked and saw a Pious man. And I found his piety repulsive.

The man was a White One, with great wealth and a large family, and he spent his days making offerings and sacrifices to me.

This he did because he lived in abject terror that he or one of his family might make some small error and thereby offend me and forfeit everything he had.

"Offend me?" I said. "Who does he think he is? Actually, that idea does offend me."

He is a prisoner of his fear, said the Soft Voice. *He cannot know and love you as he is, because no one can love something they are terrified of. You must heal his fear.*

"Ah!" I said. "I can see that, and I know what must be done."

2

So I went to the man as the Lord of Chaos, the Red One, and took from him everything that was dear to him.

Gone was his wealth, gone was his family, and gone was his health.

Now he is ready, said the Soft Voice. *Now nothing stands between you and him. Now watch and see!*

3

The man's friends came to him to comfort him.

"You have done something wrong," they told him. "You have sinned against God and offended him in some way."

When I heard this, the Red Mist started to descend, but the Soft Voice said, *Wait and watch. All of this is part of the healing.*

The man's friends continued to come to him and try to deceive him, but he held fast.

"It is God that does this," he said. "Who else could it be? I don't know why he does it, but he does."

4

The friends continued to come, and the man's wife joined them.

"You coward!" she said. "Why don't you do something! Just curse God and die."

The man held fast, but he was driven to his knees by the torment.

Finally, in desperation, he cried out to me, "Show yourself! It is you who does all these things to me. You wound me without cause, and torment me! Show yourself, you God damned fucking asshole!"

At last! said the Soft Voice. *Are you offended?*

"Of course not," I said. "He really doesn't have that kind of power. Because it's not possible for him to call me something that I am not.

"Now he is ready."

5

I then came to the man and showed myself to him as I AM.

The man was emptied of himself. The person that he had been was annihilated, and what was left was a new creation.

No longer was he afraid of me. Now he knew me, and loved me with his Whole Heart.

His health, his wealth, and his family were restored to him, and he lived out his days in communion with me.

The Seventh Book
of Yahweh
Called
Jonah

1

I had a Prophet, a man who spoke to the People for me. This Prophet was filled with rage, and burned with righteous indignation at a City.

This City was filled with wickedness and Evil. Its inhabitants spent their days in excesses of the flesh, and they had no regard for me.

The Prophet, who was a White One, was about to be consumed by the fire of his rage, so the Soft Voice said to me, *You must heal them both. You must heal the Prophet, and you must heal the City.*

2

So I spoke to my Prophet and told him that he must go the City and preach against it and that the fire of his anger would bring those people to me.

But the Prophet was afraid of the task I had given him and fled in another direction.

His fear drives him away from your healing grace, said the Soft Voice. *You cannot allow this.*

Heeding the Soft Voice, I then cast the Prophet into darkness, so that his vision might be made clear.

And the Prophet remained in the darkness until he was able to see.

3

The Prophet then went to the City and preached my Words. And the Words were Fire and Brimstone on the heads of the inhabitants.

The leaders of the City and its inhabitants then turned from their Evil ways, and came to me.

But the anger of the Prophet still burned with a fierce intensity at the past wrongs.

You must let him burn until he is fully cooked, said the Soft Voice.

This I did, and when the Prophet had
been refined by the fire of his own anger, I
went to him as the Soft Voice.

Why were you born? I asked. *What is your
purpose? Without the City and its Evil, you would
have had no reason to live. Your task was
accomplished, and the City was delivered. Your Whole
Life has come from this.*

*Both you and the City have been brought to me by
Evil.*

"I see!" said the Prophet. "Now I not
only speak with your voice, but I see with your
eyes. Evil is good!

Yes, I said. *Now you see!*

The Eighth Book
of Yahweh
Called
Jesus

1

The People were living under the rule of a powerful Empire. The Empire was governed by Red Ones, and the People were abused and oppressed. The time had come for another messiah.

He will be a White One, I said. *And he will be a Deceiver.*

The White Ones will see him as a Savior. For they will see part of me in him, and believe it to be the Whole. They will thus be saved from meeting me as I AM.

Many of the Red Ones will sell their birthrights to him for a bowl of his pottage. But his pottage will not nourish them.
For them, he will be a stumbling block and a Heel Grabber. They will find themselves cast out, and

they will have difficult lives, filled with Chaos and suffering.

Both the Red Ones and the White Ones will receive the blessing they must have for the continuation of Creation. For I am perfect.

In time there will be some men and women, both Red and White, who will reclaim their birthrights. They will meet me in the Fire as I AM, and become as I AM.

After that, it will be my voice they speak with and my eyes they see with. It will be my hands they work with, and my feet they walk with.

2

There was at that time a young woman of the People who was great with child. She had not yet married, so the Chosen One would have no father.

I saw that the child's father was a Red One. A soldier of the Empire.

Ah! Once again it is so, I said. *The mighty Empire has sown the seeds of its own downfall.*

For this messiah will conquer the Empire as the Prince of Peace.

3

The young woman had a cousin who was also with child. She was carrying a Red One.

When the two mothers met, the children recognized each other in their wombs, and the Red One leapt for joy at the Good News.

4

After the birth of the Savior there began, once again, the Slaughter of the Innocents.

As always, it was I who did this to provide food for what was to come.

And the spirits of the Innocents returned to me.

I had warned the Mother of the Child about the coming holocaust in a dream, so she and her husband-to-be took the Child south to the Land of Plenty where they remained until I told them it was safe to return to their home.

5

After returning home, the Child grew to young manhood among the People. And he amazed the Priests and Elders with his knowledge of my ways.

His interpretation of the Scriptures astounded them, and he told them things that were not written in any book. For he knew many things he had never been taught.

When the time came for the beginning of his ministry, I took him to his Red Cousin for his initiation.

The Red One took him into the Waters, and there the Two became One.

After this, I took the Son of Man into the Desert where he met me as I AM, and he became the Savior.

6

Returning from the Desert, the Savior began to preach the Good News, telling everyone that my Kingdom was at hand.

The White Ones, however, could not understand that he meant It was already spread out upon the earth, so he began to teach in parables, speaking into the understanding of the People.

The Savior then began performing feats of magic and miracles of healing by means of my power.

And the People loved him, and the number of his followers grew.

7

The Savior gathered around him an inner circle of twelve followers who lived with him, traveled with him and to whom he gave close instruction as to the nature of his Being, and the reason for his coming.

Among these twelve were two Red Ones. The mission of the ten White Disciples was to carry the message of hope and forgiveness to the masses of people that would come to follow him. The mission of one of the Red Ones was to arrange his passage to the Tree of Life where he would meet me and become as I AM.

The mission of the other Red Disciple was to carry another, very different, version of the Good News to Red Ones in the world. A message that would nourish them in accordance with the blessing that they had been given.

8

The number of the Savior's followers continued to grow. As word of magic and miracles spread, the tiny cult grew to be a Movement.

The priests and officials of the temple began to fear the power of the Savior, because he threatened their authority, their standing in the community, and their very livelihoods. They began to plot against him.

It is perfect. All is as it should be. As always, the one that they cast out will become the cornerstone for a new branch of my Creation.

The officials of the temple began to foster unrest among the People. This soon came to the attention of the officials of the Empire, who had a very low tolerance for Chaos in their realm.

9

The Priesthood then contracted with the Red Disciple for the delivery of the Savior into the hands of the soldiers of the Empire.

The Red Disciple accomplished the task that I had given him and the Savior was arrested and imprisoned.

The Savior was then brought before a Governor of the Empire, who examined him.

The Governor could find no wrong that the Savior had done, because the Savior had in fact done no wrong.

The Governor would have released the Savior, but the Priesthood protested so violently that the Governor, fearing Chaos, agreed to deliver the Savior to them so that they might do with him what they willed.

The piety of the Priesthood made them afraid to kill the Savior themselves, so they demanded that the Empire do this for them.

The Governor agreed to do this.

10

The Savior was then tortured by the soldiers of the Empire and taken to the Tree of Life, where he gave himself back to me and returned to me as I AM.

The Empire, having done as I wished, had unknowingly loosed a Power much greater than it was.

In the Chaos that followed, the Movement was solidified to such an extent that it would outlive the Empire by millennia as an agent for Good and Evil in my Creation.

The Ninth Book
of Yahweh
Called
Revelation

1

After the death of the Savior, my vision became like crystal. His death, and his experience at the Tree of Life, changed me.

All at once, things that I had only seen partially became incredibly clear to me.

This clarity was so bright and clean that it melted solid rock.

My Creation appeared in its perfection as it had always been, spread out over the earth, with my Garden at its center. But now it shone like a jewel.

Hatred and greed appeared to me as they were: illusions.

No longer was I a jealous God, for if I am the only one here, who is there to be jealous of? As with everything else, the other gods have always been multifarious reflections of me. And I in turn am nothing more than a reflection of them.

I saw myself in a way that I never had before. I saw myself as the Whole. All was in me, and I was in All, with nothing omitted.

Now, not only do I see myself in this way, I see you in this way as well. Now, not only am I a reflection of you, you are a reflection of me. We are both the "Both/And".

> *I am both God and Man.*
> *And so are you.*
> *I am both good and evil.*
> *And so are you.*
> *I am both male and female.*
> *And so are you.*
> *I am both temporal and eternal.*
> *And so are you.*
> *I am both the Red One and the White One.*
> *And so are you.*

> *I am the only one here.*
> *And so are you.*

2

Gone are sin and death. Gone is any need for forgiveness or redemption. Gone are the diseases of guilt and shame.

As it was in the beginning, is now and ever shall be, world without end, Amen.

61

Allen Proctor is a Spiritual Director, Presbyterian Minister, and Director of the Haden Institute.

His formal education was at Davidson College, Columbia Seminary, Union Seminary New York, and Gordon-Conwell Seminary.

Throughout his ministry he has worked with others on questions of identity, relationships, vocation and meaning, using dreamwork, the Enneagram, Myers-Briggs Type Indicator, meditation practices, and Celtic spirituality.

Rev. Stephen Herring has a passion for the philosophy of education and religion. He is a community college instructor in geography and comparative religions. He also serves as supply pastor for two Presbyterian churches.

His academic background is primarily in biblical studies and classical languages. He holds an M.Div. degree from Yale University (1983) and a BA in Classical Studies from the University of California at Santa Cruz (1980).

Rawls Howard is a provincial American Southerner. Since the close of his small consulting business in 2001, he has devoted himself to the cultivation of his spiritual growth.

He has ongoing relationships with the church, Alcoholics Anonymous, and the Haden Institute.

This book is his fourth.

He holds a BS degree in business and accounting from the University of North Carolina at Wilmington (1971) and a certificate in Spiritual Formation from the Haden Institute (2019).